NEW YORK VOICES
OLD FRIENDS

TABLE OF CONTENTS

Front Cover:
Photo by Peter Blum

Back Cover:
Sketch by Peter Eldridge
Photos by Chris Carroll

ISBN 978-1-4803-6227-7

SHAWNEE PRESS

EXCLUSIVELY DISTRIBUTED BY

HAL•LEONARD®
CORPORATION

7777 W. BLUEMOUND RD. P.O. BOX 13819 MILWAUKEE, WI 53213

Visit Shawnee Press Online at
www.shawneepress.com

Visit Hal Leonard Online at
www.halleonard.com

FOREWORD

Photo: Janis Wilkins

It gives me the greatest of pleasures to write a few words about my "old friends," The New York Voices: Kim, Darmon, Peter, and Lauren, and this collection of their vocal arrangements. As a member of The Manhattan Transfer and a vocal arranger myself, I am a student and aficionado of the sacred art of arranging voices in harmony. It's not everybody who can write down vocal parts and have them really "sing," no matter how accomplished a musician you are. The lineage of this art form stretches back to groups like The Boswell Sisters and The Rhythm Boys, and to the great harmony groups within the big bands, such as the Pied Pipers, Merry Macs and the Modernaires.

There is a noble history. A great arrangement sung well will plumb the depths of a song and bring the listener closer to that heaven of musical transcendence. Kim, Darmon, Peter, and Lauren have my greatest and most heartfelt admiration for not only being superlative vocal musicians and keepers of the flame, but masters at the craft of arranging voices. The songs in this collection are standards on many levels...some traditional like "I'll Be Seeing You" and "Sing, Sing, Sing," Paul Simon classics from a younger generation, as well as Ellington's "Bli-Blip," and a Peter Eldridge original.

Now you can sing these incredible jazz vocal orchestrations that have been lovingly crafted by New York Voices.

Enjoy, have fun and "Sing, Sing, Sing."
Janis Siegel
New York City

This book is dedicated to our mentor, teacher, fellow arranger, and friend, David J. Riley.

(Dec. 9, 1931 - Feb. 23, 2015)

Dave's passion and guidance for vocal jazz at Ithaca College pulled us all together for an experience that has lasted a lifetime. He was generous enough to give us our very first tour in Europe at the North Sea and Montreux Jazz Festivals that fateful summer of 1986, and then again as a guest with his college choir at Town Hall in New York City on February 2, 1988. This is the date we celebrate our New York Voices Anniversary, and will continue to remember the man who changed our lives. He was a proud member of the audience at the Kennedy Center, at Symphony Hall with the Boston Pops, our 25th Anniversary performance at the Jazz Standard, and our New York Voices Vocal Jazz Camp in Ohio. We can only hope that those of you singing this music are as deeply affected, inspired, and supported by your directors, as we were by ours. We are better teachers, arrangers, conductors, performers, and people for knowing him. There would have been no New York Voices without Dave Riley, for he gave us our name. This one's for you, Dave, "Old Friend," we love you.

Your New York Voices,
Kim, Peter, Darmon and Lauren

Photo: Peter Blum

We, the New York Voices, would like to take this opportunity to thank all of you responsible for helping us sustain our long career as musicians, performers, arrangers, composers, teachers, clinicians and adjudicators. Without you, there would be no need for this exciting collection of arrangements that we hope brings some ease to your music gathering and selection process. Please enjoy the photos, captions, and quips written especially for you, so your understanding of our approach is that much clearer. Recorded and live performances of these pieces can be found on our website, and rhythm parts are available as digital downloads at shawneepress.com. You may contact any one of us at newyorkvoices.com should you need additional help or have specific questions.

This book is a dream come true for us, and another milestone in our musical journey. We'd especially like to thank Greg Gilpin and his staff at Hal Leonard/Shawnee Press for their willingness, dedication and patience as we navigated through these new business waters. And our eternal thanks to Kate Kooser, for tying up all of the loose ends, and truly helping to make this vision a reality!

We're with you in spirit as you rehearse, pound notes, discover harmonies, embrace rhythms and make this music your own! Any chart is simply a guide to your individual and unique expression of the music. Please remember to have fun in the process. Some of the best music making happens in the choir room, classroom, and practice room. We hope you, too, become "Old Friends" through the music in your lives. We're glad we could be a small part of it.

Kim Nazarian, Lauren Kinhan, Peter Eldridge, and Darmon Meader
NEW YORK VOICES

Ian Ashby (Kim's son), 2 years old (2002), at the wheel of the NYV tour bus in Germany - a seasoned "Baby Driver!"

The group was in the 'eleventh hour' of recording our album of Paul Simon songs, which was provocatively entitled *New York Voices Sing the Songs of Paul Simon* - it seems that was the only title we were allowed to use! Our label at the time, RCA Victor, said we needed a rollicking swinger to open the project, since most of the album was a significant departure from the usual New York Voices fare. Darmon was fairly tapped out from all of the duties the project had already thrown at him, so I was asked to put something together at the last minute. I remembered this quirky, energetic shuffle called 'Baby Driver' (off the *Bridge Over Troubled Water* album) and thought it might fit the bill. I put the main part of the arrangement together in the wee hours of the morning, then Darmon came in to add final tweaks before we went into the studio (the next day!) to record it. Until then, the group had never arranged, learned and recorded a tune so fast in our lives. It was stressful, but it worked. Since then, the song has grown and become even more robust and swinging in live performance. I have always wanted to publicly apologize for the wacky rhythm of the intro line. It's not for the squeamish. **Peter**

BABY DRIVER

for SATB and Piano, with Optional Rhythm Section Accompaniment*
Duration: ca. 3:40

**Arranged by PETER ELDRIDGE
and DARMON MEADER**

Words and Music by
PAUL SIMON

* **Rhythm parts available via digital download (35030698)**
(pno, b, dm)
www.shawneepress.com

New York Voices performing in a church in Warsaw, Poland. Winter 2012.

While doing research for the *Sing! Sing! Sing!* project, I was listening to an Ellington collection and stumbled on "Bli-Blip." The tune itself is relatively simple, but charming. What really caught my ear was the quirky shout chorus. I transcribed that section, and added lyrics. This became the "No I never" section that follows the solos. For the recording, Michael Abene added a great seven-horn accompaniment, which has some additional sections that do not appear in this published version. However, the song works great with just trio accompaniment, and is a great improvisation vehicle with relatively simple but hearty chord changes. This song has been a staple in our shows for many years. ***Darmon***

BLI-BLIP

For SATB and Piano with Optional Rhythm Section Accompaniment*
Duration: ca. 6:00

Arrangement and
Additional Lyrics by
DARMON MEADER

By DUKE ELLINGTON
and SID KULLER

*Rhythm parts available via digital download (35030699)
(pno, b, dm)
www.shawneepress.com

DO NOT
PHOTOCOPY

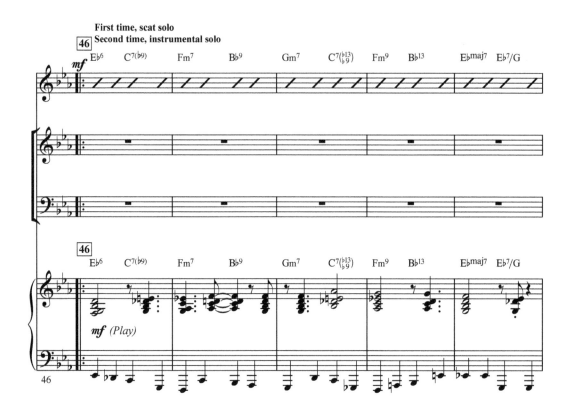

Right after I graduated from Ithaca College (where Darmon, Kim and I all sang in the vocal jazz group conducted by dear Dave Riley), I was a singing waiter at a resort hotel in New Hampshire (a 'dues paying' time in my life for sure - my parents, somewhat mockingly, liked to refer to it as a 'character-building experience'). It was a ridiculously low-paying, round-the-clock job, but it's where I met many life-long friends who taught me about the concept of 'work family' (thus preparing me for life as a New York Voice). Susan (aka Smitty) Smith Cohen, who was a part of this goofy menagerie of singing plate-slingers, had shown me a poem she had written called "Come Home to Me." It was beautiful and very long, and I asked her if I could paraphrase what she had written, cut it down significantly, and set it musically. She kindly said yes. It felt like a prayer of sorts, or a very romantic calling to a loved one. I sat at my parents' piano one afternoon and wrote the piece rather quickly, not really sure what I had when I finished it. Was it a jazz piece, or sort of a contemporary classical piece? Either way, it has had a nice life with many high school, college and All-State groups over the years. Nothing makes me happier than when a group of students run up to me after a Voices' concert and ask if they could sing it for me. They're so proud and earnest and sweet. It's the best feeling. **Peter**

Photo: NYV Friend from Music Fest Canada Staff

New York Voices in the cold snowfall at Banff National Park, Alberta, Canada. April, 2009.

COME HOME

for SATB a cappella

Duration: ca. 2:15

**Words by PETER ELDRIDGE
and SUSAN SMITH COHEN**

**Music by
PETER ELDRIDGE**

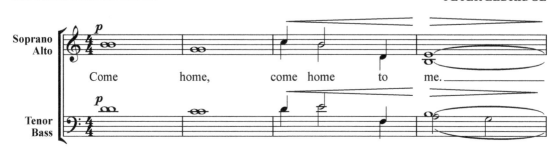

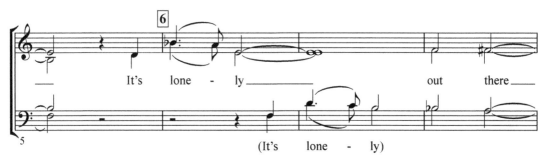

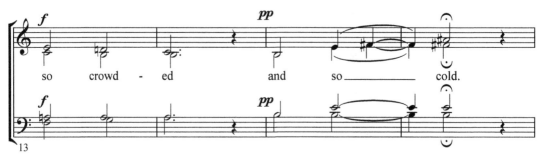

Peter Eldridge and his late father, Charles Cummings, enjoying a jazz cruise in Scandinavia, 2007.
Charlie is checking his watch for the warm waffles that appeared on deck at 4 pm daily!

Photos: Darmon Meador

When I think of the evolution of this arrangement, for me it begins and ends with my son. I was pregnant when we recorded this on the *Sing! Sing! Sing!* CD, and I remember having to focus on the longer phrases because of the obvious obstruction to my breathing! To be perfectly honest, we did record to a piano guide track to keep us right on target. When we were in the editing room all together, the way we focused on every intimate detail as a team was so cool. If I may quote Darmon Meader: "the use of rubato should take the same amount of time, as if you sang the piece in a constant tempo." In other words, please find places where you can move forward, as well as slow down. We also encourage you to embrace the modulation with care - don't over sing it. Personally, the most memorable performances of this poignant song were directly after the 9/11 tragedy (could hardly get through it), and the memorial service for Peter's Dad, the incomparable Charles Cummings. With each future performance, I dedicate the music to those we've lost and to seeing my son and family again when I return home from tour. This song belongs to all of us in one way or another. It is our sincere pleasure to share the moving experience of singing this arrangement with others, to others, and for others. *Kim*

I'LL BE SEEING YOU

for SATB (w/optional divisi) a cappella

Duration: ca. 3:50

Arranged by
DARMON MEADER

Written by **IRVING KAHAL**
and **SAMMY FAIN**

*No breath

When searching through the Paul Simon repertoire for possible tunes for the NYV record-ing, I thought this tune would lend itself nicely to a samba groove and work as a female lead. The "Late in the Evening" quote served a dual purpose in providing the New York Voices signature instrumental influence, while introducing another Simon song. I remember sitting with Darmon one afternoon working on the Harry Belafonte call and response section, and laughing about all of the satisfying modulations in this chart! It was a thrill to see Peter Calo on guitar and Cyro Baptiste on percussion lay down this track in the studio. It was the first time I had seen that type of Brazilian clapping in action, and heard the cuíca with a humorous lick-not to mention Darmon's super sax solo! It took us two separate sessions to get the vocals right on this tune. We find that live performance legs go a long way before recording new material.

We recommend that you perform this chart a little slower than our recorded version, and watch out for the odd meters at the end. A few friendly tips: think in a big two for the rhythm; feel the upbeats; DON'T RUSH; and go for a smooth, forward moving line. New York Voices has performed this song in both the trio and orchestral settings; no matter the accompani-ment, this chart is a pleaser for both performer and listener. ENJOY!! *Kim*

Photo: Montreal Jazz Fest Photographer

New York Voices at the Montreal Jazz Festival in 1998 with special guests (from left to right);
Gil Goldstein, Valcino, Peter Calo, Christian McBride, and Andy Ezrin.
To date, this is our favorite documented performance of the Paul Simon repertoire.

ME AND JULIO
DOWN BY THE SCHOOLYARD

for SATB and Piano with Optional Rhythm Section Accompaniment*
Duration: ca 4:05

**Arranged by
DARMON MEADER**

**Words and Music by
PAUL SIMON**

* **Available Separately:**
Rhythm parts (35014041) (b, dm)
www.shawneepress.com

**DO NOT
PHOTOCOPY**

*Instrumental or scat solo. (Tenor sax solo on original recording.)

Kim and Marge Nazarian (Kim's dearly departed Mother, March 18, 2015) nestled in the coastline of Sweden. (2007)

I have always found this song of Paul's to be quite an enigma. There are more than a few different theories as to what it's about exactly. Some say it is the story of a custody battle of a child in a court hearing (and quite literal with the line 'the mother and child reunion is only a motion away'), some report that 'mother and child reunion' is a dish at a Chinese restaurant, and there are still others who say the song is about the death of a family dog. But either way, in Paul's original version, the energetic reggae groove and the ebullient background vocals lie in stark contrast with the lyric. I tend to go for the more bittersweet side of music (generally speaking) and definitely went in that direction for this arrangement. I came up with the piano intro line and basic re-harmonization first as a musical anchor and, uncharacteristically for New York Voices, put the melody in the bottom voice. Darmon came in and helped me voice out some elements here and there. No matter what the song is ultimately about, it always seems to resonate with people. Vince Mendoza did an incredible job orchestrating the piece when we first performed it with Netherland's Metropole Orchestra many years ago. I will never forget feeling like the luckiest person in the world the first time we rehearsed it with that incredible group of musicians, sitting at the piano surrounded by the string section, and realizing life probably wouldn't get any better than that. **Peter**

PERFORMANCE NOTES

This arrangement, based on the New York Voices' recorded arrangement of Paul Simon's hit song, is a cut on "New York Voices Sing the Songs of Paul Simon" (RCA B000003GAH). Portions of the baritone part are suitable for a solo voice, while other portions can be sung by the section to blend with the choir. If sung as a solo, the singer should listen to the recording and feel free to ad lib. tastefully.

Your performance can be greatly enhanced by including the guitar, bass, and drums parts available from the publisher (35027150). Starting at measure 64, and continuing to measure 81, the guitar part simulates the great guitar solo played on the recording by Marc Shulman. For those choirs that do not have extra instrumentalists for these 17 measures, an *ossia* part is written for the accompanist to play on the keyboard.

Ossia, in Italian, means, literally, *or.* The accompanist plays the regular (larger) staffs at measure 64 when there is a guitarist available to play the solo. *Or* if there is no guitarist, the solo can be given to the accompanist, who may play either the solo written on the ossia (smaller) staffs, or create his/her own solo based on the chords shown. *Or* you may have an adventurous musician who would like to play the solo on another instrument.

MOTHER AND CHILD REUNION

for SATB and Piano with Optional Rhythm Section Accompaniment*
Duration: ca. 5:10

Arranged by
**PETER ELDRIDGE and
DARMON MEADER**

Words and Music by
PAUL SIMON

* Rhythm parts available as a digital download (35027150)
(gtr, b, dm)
www.shawneepress.com

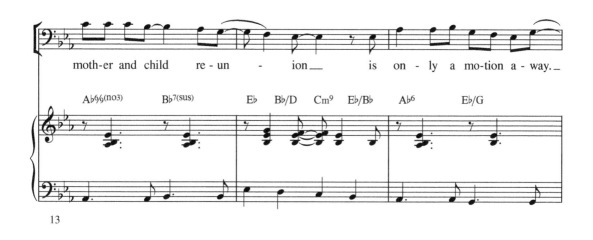

*In absence of guitar solo, the accompanist may play the ossia staffs, or there may be an ad lib. solo. See page 73.

Old Friends

Old Friends

The line that always gets to me is, "I have a photograph, preserve your memories, they're all that's left you." There is something so final about that. It reminds us to live in the present, pay attention to the ones you love and the life you are living, so when you do finally get to that place in your life, you will have a bounty of memories to reminisce about while sitting on that "park bench." This song is also an affirmation of our musical family and the experiences we've shared together; a reminder of how profound friendships can impact our lives. **Lauren**

I must say this dark, moody Paul Simon song has had some powerful live performances – the Montreal Jazz Festival comes immediately to mind. The silence when we were finished singing was long and profound, like no one in the audience wanted to leave the moment created. In my humble opinion, Darmon and Gil Goldstein's stark, sweet arrangement gives the song a perfect setting. **Peter**

I hope we are still singing together when we're 70! This book is just what the lyrics describe: an attempt to preserve our musical memories. **Kim**

This is still one of my favorites to sing. Though recorded with an instrumental quartet, we perform the "Old Friends" section a cappella on our live gigs. Then we have our pianist improvise the interlude, bringing us back to the "Bookends" section. Over the years, we've had many pianists perform this with us, and some magical moments have transpired. **Darmon**

Photo: Roberto Citarelli

OLD FRIENDS/BOOKENDS

For SATB and Piano
Duration: ca. 5:36

Arranged by
DARMON MEADER

Words and Music by
PAUL SIMON

brush - es the same years,

si - lent-ly shar - ing the same fears.

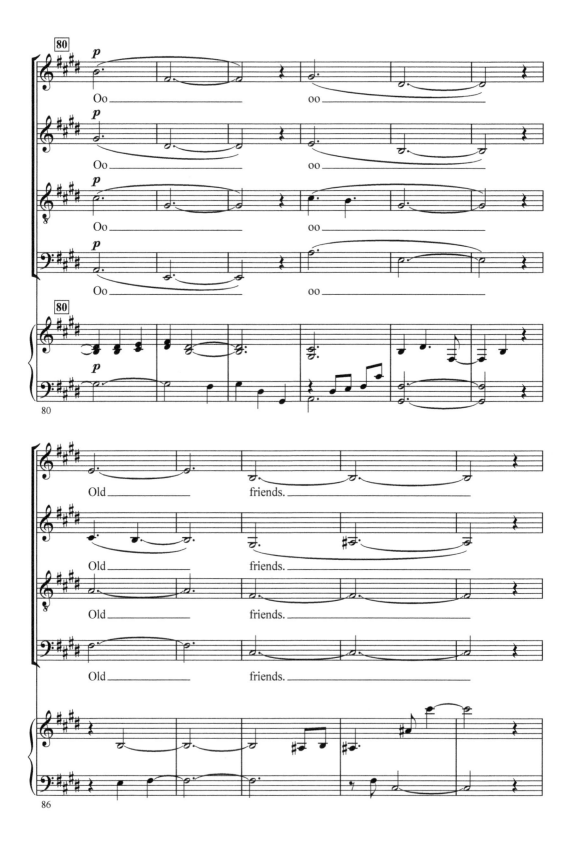

When picking repertoire, NYV has often gravitated to lesser-known songs. This was somewhat true when we were picking our songs for our *Sing! Sing! Sing!* big band project, so we needed to add a couple of "A-list" swing tunes to the CD. "Sing, Sing, Sing" definitely fit the bill, but since the song has been in heavy rotation since the 30's, we felt it was imperative that we really mix it up to make our version unique. At the same time, we didn't want to ditch the swing energy that is so key to this song. So, my arrangement bounces back and forth between traditional harmony and more "tweaked" altered harmony to freshen up the song. Over the years this has become one of our "hits" (if there is such a thing in vocal jazz?!), and we have had the pleasure of performing it all over the world in many beautiful venues, with wonderful trios, big bands and symphonies galore. ***Darmon***

U.S. Air Force Photo

New York Voices with the prestigious Airmen of Note. September, 2009.

SING, SING, SING

for SATB and Piano with Optional Instrumental Accompaniment*
Duration: ca. 4:45

Arranged by
DARMON MEADER

Words and Music by **LOUIS PRIMA**
Additional Lyrics by **PETER ELDRIDGE**
and **DARMON MEADER**

*Available separately:
Rhythm parts (35020346) (b, dm)
Big Band parts (35020345)
(asx 1,2, tsx 1,2, barsx, tpt 1,2,3, tbn 1,2,3, btbn, b, dm, pno)
www.shawneepress.com

Jesse Stone, working under his pseudonym, Charles A. Calhoun, wrote the hard swinging tune "Smack Dab in the Middle." It has been covered by many famous artists including Joe Williams and Ray Charles. In addition to paying homage to primarily the Charles version, Darmon wrote a shout section that broke up the verse-chorus form; I had fun writing lyrics for this section that stayed in tune with the overall vibe of the song. We built in a traditional call and response between us and the recorded Big Band, later credited The Rob Marcus Singers. Don't bother searching the lineage of that singing group, as some fans have done already; it was named after my husband who was invited to sing with the Big Band on the recording date. He took it quite seriously, situating himself right up on the mic, and permanently becoming a prominent voice in what was otherwise supposed to be the group shout out. It remains a crowd favorite and a mainstay in our live show, with Darmon and I inviting the audience to sing along with us "Smack Dab in the Middle" of the song and at the very end. It's a dynamic arrangement with lots of room for explosive, surprising moments and super quiet break downs that build right back up again. Have fun with it and good luck. **Lauren**

New York Voices photo shoot in Köln, Germany.

Photo: Peter Blum

SMACK DAB IN THE MIDDLE

for SATB and Piano with Optional Instrumental Accompaniment*
Duration: ca. 5:10

**Arranged by
DARMON MEADER**

**Words and Music by
CHARLES E. CALHOUN
Additional Lyrics by
LAUREN KINHAN and DARMON MEADER**

* **Available Separately:**
Big Band parts (35020685)
(asx 1,2, tsx 1,2, barsx, tpt 1,2,3,4, tbn 1,2,3,4, b, dm, pno)
www.shawneepress.com

jel - ly roll_ me   smack dab_ in the mid - dle of it all._

Come an' find me,   wine an' dine me,   and let me

rock an' roll to   soothe my soul._____

Smack Dab In the Middle

look at the mess I'm in, it's a mor-al ep-i-dem-ic, they say.

When the drum-mer sets the feet to fly-in', front an' cen-ter's

where I'll be. Don't knock it if you nev-er would, ev-er could. An-y-one, an-y-where

Smack Dab In the Middle

151

Darmon Meader on the beach in Rio de Janeiro, November, 2008.

Our Paul Simon project was the most collaborative arranging venture in our career. "Why Don't You Write Me?" is a perfect example of four sensibilities and a multitude of ideas and laughter being thrown into one soup pot and stirring! We liked the wit and wink of the lyric even though it's storied to be a song Paul wrote while missing his wife on the road. Simon is a master of transporting us with his songwriting, often laying a heavy text on a light and lively bed of music, thus the listener doesn't often realize the tune might be a lament of some kind. And here, we just took the wink, and added more! We amplified elements of his arrangement, like the "La La La" line and used it as fodder for a recurring theme. And we played with going from one groove to another as a way to flex our own mischievous muscles. If you are a fan of how this chart narrowly walks that line of fun and technique, that's exactly what is required to keep it solidly on the track and not just a joke. So make sure you take the time to finesse the close harmonies and practice the transitions. The listener, not you, should be taken on a surprising ride! We had fun coming up with quotes at the end of the song referencing letter writing, feel free to come up with some of your own. And by all means, have fun. *Lauren*

WHY DON'T YOU WRITE ME?

for SATB and Piano with Optional Instrumental Accompaniment*
Duration: ca. 3:15

Arranged by
**DARMON MEADER, PETER ELDRIDGE,
LAUREN KINHAN and KIM NAZARIAN**

Words and Music by
PAUL SIMON

*Available Separately: SATB (35025868)
Rhythm parts available as a digital download
(b, dm)
www.shawneepress.com

*No breath

*No breath

*This phrase sung "tongue in cheek—overly-classical"

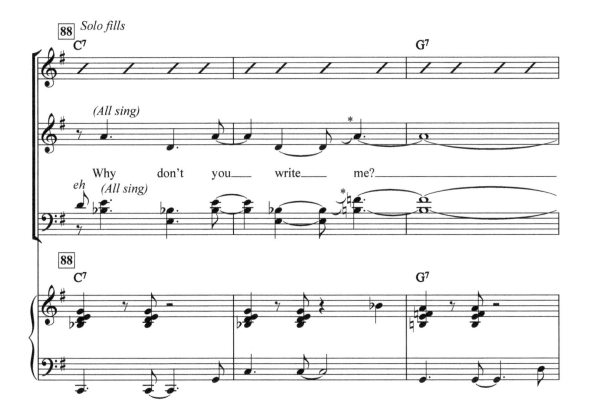

*Bend up to note.

Why don't you___ write___ me?___

Send me a let-ter, if on-ly to tell me you're plan-ning to send me a let - ter.___